THEN & NOW

PLYMOUTH

Opposite: This *c.* 1930 view is from Main Street looking down Union Street toward the Daisy Manufacturing Company. Only the front wall of the main building on the right stands today.

PLYMOUTH

Brian Vincent Hill
for the Plymouth Historical Society

This book is dedicated to the memory of Sam Hudson Jr. (1922–1988). Hudson, born in Salford, England, relocated from New York City to the Plymouth area in the 1950s. Through his personal interest in history, Hudson became a part-time columnist for the Plymouth Observer newspaper, writing articles on Plymouth's history, which eventually served as the foundation for his 1976 book, The Story of Plymouth, Michigan: A Midwest Microcosm. *Hudson also produced a then and now photographic book,* Plymouth in Pictures: Past and Present, *in 1972. In his time, Hudson was known as the foremost authority on Plymouth's history and an outstanding volunteer who helped further the cause of education and the importance of preserving local history.*

Library of Congress Control Number: 2009925358

Published by Arcadia Publishing
Charleston SC, Chicago IL, Portsmouth NH, San Francisco CA

Printed in the United States of America

For all general information contact Arcadia Publishing at:
Telephone 843-853-2070
Fax 843-853-0044
E-mail sales@arcadiapublishing.com
For customer service and orders:
Toll-Free 1-888-313-2665

Visit us on the Internet at www.arcadiapublishing.com

On the front cover: These photographs contrast the look of the main business block on Main Street in front of Kellogg Park over 100 years, from 1900 to 2008. (Vintage photograph courtesy of the Plymouth Historical Society; contemporary photograph by Bryan Vincent Hill.)

On the back cover: Automobiles and horse and buggies share Penniman Avenue in this photograph from about 1920. (Courtesy of the Plymouth Historical Society.)

CONTENTS

ACKNOWLEDGMENTS

As is the case with any undertaking such as this, many people stand behind each page, whether through direct assistance, inspiration, or moral support. The genesis of this book took place after purchasing the second addition of Sam Hudson's *Plymouth in Pictures: Past and Present*. In the early 1970s, Hudson did an excellent job of showcasing images of contemporary Plymouth juxtaposed with similar images from the late 19th century and early 20th century. My goal was to update his work with similar images from early-21st-century Plymouth. My work was aided tremendously by Liz Kerstens, executive director of the Plymouth Historical Society. She previously published two books through Arcadia about Plymouth. Through her influence, I also became a volunteer at the Plymouth Historical Society and ultimately editor of its newsletter.

Many fine people associated with the society have helped me pull everything together. Garry Packard was my early archives guide and weekend research partner. Plymouth Historical Society president emeritus Sanford Burr has been an inexhaustible source of Plymouth history not to mention an excellent storyteller and perfect example of a true Plymouth pedigree. James Curtiss, owner of the Tibbitts house and barn, provided me with fascinating articles and stories about early Plymouth and the Tibbitts family. Wendy Harless, chairperson of the Plymouth Preservation Network (www.plymouthpreservation.org), supplied me with many excellent articles and images previously compiled by the Plymouth-Canton branch of the American Association of University Women (AAUW). And Heidi Nielsen, archivist for the Plymouth Historical Society, was a great help in locating and scanning old photographs from the Plymouth area.

Not to forget, thank you to my patient wife and children, who put up with my constant photograph excursions, weekend trips to the museum, and late nights on the computer.

Thanks to you all and enjoy!

All vintage images appear courtesy of the Plymouth Historical Society, and all contemporary images were photographed by the author.

Hill, Brian Vincent. *Plymouth*. Plymouth: Plymouth Historical Society, 2009. ix.

INTRODUCTION

The story of Plymouth at first glance is unremarkably similar to many of the early southeastern Michigan towns that sprang up after the opening of the Erie Canal in 1826. The first pioneers primarily came from the New England area and made their way here from New York via the recently opened canal. Plymouth Township was first settled in 1824, and today's city of Plymouth was in 1825. The area formerly known as Section T1S-R8E was named by settlers as Plymouth Township in 1827. The village of Plymouth separated from the township and incorporated in 1867, and became the city of Plymouth in 1932. The year 1867 is recognized as the official date the city of Plymouth was founded. At first, Plymouth consisted mostly of trees, wild animals, sporadic Native American encounters, log cabins, and new farms. A classic frontier town sprang up along an all-dirt Main Street, and a couple of churches were built along Church Street. The late 1800s brought the railroads, the development of Old Village, and manufacturing to Plymouth, yet most citizens were still engaged in agricultural pursuits. Over time, the improvement of the railroad, interurban rail system, roads, and eventual highways positioned Plymouth as a convenient suburb to Detroit's thriving automobile and manufacturing industries. The farms disappeared, as did the local industry, and Plymouth simply became known as a quaint place to live, shop, and dine.

Like many small towns, underneath the quaint exterior lies a rich history of courage, genius, heartache, scandal, and success that makes Plymouth much more than an idyllic image from a Thomas Kincaid painting. The story of Then and Now: *Plymouth* has something for everyone. Enjoy!

HOME SWEET HOME

The house at 1279 West Ann Arbor Trail may be the oldest still standing in the city of Plymouth. Timothy Lyons built this L-shaped farmhouse around 1827, and in the early 1960s, the house's exterior was extensively remodeled (seen here) and moved farther back on the property by new owner and local architect Thomas Moss.

John Tibbitts house, built about 1827, is located at 46225 North Territorial Road. Some believe that this is the oldest-standing house in Plymouth. The barn where the early settlers chose Plymouth's name in 1827 still stands on the property, as well as an old milk house. This classic L-shaped farmhouse replaced an earlier log cabin and was renovated in the Greek Revival style by the third homeowners—Earl and Elizabeth Demel—in 1939. The historic view below is from the 1960s.

Pumpkin Hill house at 187 Adams Street was built about 1834. This may be the oldest house in the city of Plymouth on its original foundation. Vanita Adams, for whom Adams Street is named, lived in this house for 40 years. The home's present-day namesake comes from one of its later owners, Sandra Richards, who restored it in the late 1970s (seen here) and whose birthday fell on October 31.

The Penniman-Allen house at 1160 Penniman Avenue was built about 1840 by Ebenezer Jenckes Penniman, the first Plymouth citizen to be elected to the United States Congress. Penniman's daughter Kate and her husband, W. O. Allen, remodeled the house in the late 1920s, adding the pillars, French doors at the front of the house, and the sun room on the east side. The house and property were sold to the Catholic church after Kate's death in 1943. The historic photograph was taken about 1900.

The Holbrook–Old Wilcox house was built about 1840 at 1142 Holbrook Street. Henry Holbrook platted the village of Plymouth in 1837, and the street is named after him. Brothers David and John (Jack) Wilcox, purchased the house in 1879 along with 320 acres of farmland that contained a wood mill and gristmill—later known as Wilcox Mill. The mill stood until 1921 when Henry Ford purchased and razed it for one of his village plants. The historic photograph was taken about 1900.

Located at 921 Church Street, the Shattuck-Garlett house was built about 1841. This house has been in three locations in Plymouth. It originally was a harness shop, built by Peter Fralick, and sat where today's Penniman Gallery exists. The structure was moved to 968 Penniman Avenue (seen in the historic photograph in the late 1800s) and turned into a residence prior to 1860. It was later purchased by the Shattuck family. In 1923, it was turned around to face Church Street, its current location, by Ella Shattuck's nephew Harry.

The Burr-Tomlinson house was built about 1845 at 41350 East Ann Arbor Trail. This former farmhouse, seen in this *c.* 1900 photograph, in Plymouth Township was once owned by Plymouth pioneer Ambrose Burr, the great-grandfather of Plymouth Historical Society president emeritus Sanford Burr. The house was later owned by the Tomlinson family in the late 1800s. Burt Tomlinson remodeled the house in 1930. He also built Southworth and Gold Arbor Roads, and the subdivision that now occupies his former farm property is called Tomlinson Estates.

The Noyes–Bake house was built around 1850 by Bethuel Noyes, the first president of the village of Plymouth, and located at 705 South Main Street. In the 1920s, William and Jessie Bake purchased the farmhouse and the property that extended from South Main Street to Ann Arbor Road. The Bakes moved the house to its current location at 760 Burroughs Street and renovated it (seen here) and plotted subdivisions in the 1930s and 1940s from this acreage before moving in 1954.

The McNamara house was originally built around 1861 on Church Street and later moved to its present location at 1011 Penniman Avenue. The McNamaras purchased the house in 1967 and refurbished it. In the 1970s, they were the subject of several newspaper and magazine articles highlighting the remodel and eclectic outdoor landscaping, complete with an old railroad crossing sign. The house's interior and exterior still maintains most of its original construction and design. The historic photograph is from about 1915.

The Park-Bennett house was built around 1875 at 134 North Main Street. This Gothic Revival–style house was first occupied by James and Mary Park and later purchased by Charles (Charlie) and Carrie Bennett. Charles was known as the colorful and flamboyant worldwide traveler and salesman who introduced the Daisy Air Rifle "into practically every civilized country except Russia." He later became president of Daisy in 1920 and held this position until his death at age 94 in 1956. The historic photograph was taken around 1902.

The Henry W. Baker house was built in 1875 at 233 South Main Street. At the age of 43, Baker helped found the Plymouth Iron Windmill Company, which in 1895 became the Daisy Manufacturing Company. Baker went on to become Daisy's first president. During the 1970s, this beautiful house was painted pink and served as a beauty salon. Attorneys and former owners David Frost and Jack March completed an extensive renovation of the house in the early 1980s. The historic photograph was taken around 1900.

The George Starkweather house was built in 1875 at 711 Starkweather Street. In 1826, the city of Plymouth's first settlers, William and Kezia Starkweather, gave birth to the first white child born here, George Anson Starkweather. He became a prominent landowner, farmer, merchant, and politician, serving as a member of Michigan's legislature in 1854 and village of Plymouth president in 1898. The road he cut through his farm property in 1870 was renamed from Oak to Starkweather Street in 1907. The historic photograph was taken in 1909.

Seen in the 1965 photograph below, the Henry Root house is at 49970 West Ann Arbor Road. Roswell Root, one of Plymouth's pioneers, built a log cabin here in 1825 and later replaced it with a frame house for his wife and 10 children. Roswell's son Henry built the current house. It is reported that the tulip and cedar boards for the house came from trees in Kellogg Park. Later owners reportedly found Native American carving stones and other relics on the property.

The Clarence Hamilton house at 311 Hamilton Street was built about 1878. Hamilton built the first all-metal air rifle and then convinced company owners to start manufacturing them, and they became known as the Daisy BB gun. He later started his own BB gun company, the Hamilton Air Rifle Company, and with his son Coella, he successfully manufactured the inexpensive Hamilton .22 caliber rifle. Depot Street, where they lived, was later changed to Hamilton Street sometime in the early 1900s prior to 1924. The historic photograph was taken about 1915.

The Miller-Cassady house at 44622 North Territorial Road was built in 1875 by Marcus Miller and sold to the Cassady family in 1945. In 1955, the family sold 35 acres of property to Western Electric, who built its plant (the location of today's Office Depot on Sheldon Road), and all of the property that houses today's New England Village subdivision. In 2002, the property was sold to a developer who built the New England–style townhouses around it. The historic photograph was taken about 1965.

The Harry Robinson house at 865 Penniman Avenue was built about 1885. This commercial property, located near the intersection of Harvey Street and Penniman Avenue, was once the elegant Queen Anne–style residence of the Harry Robinson family. Robinson was a past president of the village of Plymouth who later purchased the Ashley Perrin livery stable on Sutton Street (Penniman Avenue) and provided the community with public transportation to and from the depot in his horse-drawn bus. The historic photograph was taken about 1910.

The Thomas Patterson house/Plymouth Hospital at 218 South Main Street was built in 1893 by Thomas Patterson. In 1932, sisters Lena and Alma Weist converted it to a hospital, where it operated until Lena's death in 1954. After Alma's passing 20 years later, the house was found in clean and operational fashion—all of the beds had fresh linen on them and all of the hospital instruments were cleaned and neatly arranged in their trays. The historic photograph was taken about 1940.

The Conner house at 1103 Penniman Avenue was built in 1895 by Michael Conner, who was the popular owner of the hardware store at the northwest corner of Penniman Avenue and Main Street—a building that still bears his name. Conner played the coronet and is credited with starting the first Plymouth band in the mid-1800s. He also served as village president in 1868, 1884, and 1889. Conner died in 1896 soon after this house was built. The historic photograph was taken about 1900.

The Charles Draper house at 1046 Church Street was built in 1898. Charles Draper was a local optometrist, jeweler, clock repairman, and amateur photographer. Many of Plymouth's earliest photographs were taken by him, and they are stored today at the Plymouth Historical Museum.

The former Draper home is a modest example of Queen Anne architecture. While there have been some additions and renovations through the years, Draper would have no problem recognizing his home today. The historic photograph was taken about 1902.

The stately Second Empire John Gale house at 884 Penniman Avenue was built about 1895. The house has been remodeled extensively over the years, with few remnants of its original splendor remaining. It is now known as the Coffee Bean. Gale grew up with his uncle A. B. Coleman, who constructed the Coleman building, which stood from 1896 to 1919 where today's bank building/Plymouth Play Café is located. Gale later inherited Coleman's drug and grocery business that was located in the Coleman building. The historic photograph was taken about 1920.

Seen on the left in the historic photograph from about 1915, today's 932 Bed and Breakfast was once owned by Ella Roe-Nichols, who attended the second inaugural ball of Pres. Abraham Lincoln in 1865 with her first husband, Capt. William B. Roe, an officer in the 16th Michigan Regiment in the Civil War. She and her second husband, Dr. Harrison Nichols, built this house in 1903. Today's Plymouth Chiropractic and Wellness Center (right), was built in 1910 for local businessman Elmer Chaffee.

The Markham-Wilcox house at 676 Penniman Avenue was built in 1903 by BB gun entrepreneur William "Philip" Markham allegedly for his secretary and mistress while he was still married and living in a house near the parking lot of today's Box Bar. Markham's wife died in 1910, and he married his mistress in 1911. He then sold his house to the Wilcox family and moved to Los Angeles where he became a millionaire in the real estate industry. The historic photograph was taken about 1965.

CHURCHES
AND SCHOOLS

Plymouth's sole grade school and high school and the Methodist Episcopal Church next door were destroyed in 1916 by a fire that started in the school's furnace room. They were both rebuilt the same year on their original locations. The school is home to Central Middle School today, and the church is home to Solid Rock Bible Church.

Presbyterian Church, Plymouth, Mich.

The Presbyterians began meeting in Plymouth in private homes in 1835 and built the village's first church in 1837. A new brick building replaced it in 1846, and it burned down in 1936. The only untouched items in the fire were the Bible and the lectern, which still exist today. The church was rebuilt on roughly the same site and reopened in 1937. The chapel was added in 1955 and an educational wing was built in 2002. This photograph is likely from the 1950s.

CHURCHES AND SCHOOLS

Members of the Methodist Episcopal Church began meeting in Plymouth in private homes as early as 1828 and built their first church in 1848, close to the site of today's Solid Rock Bible Church next to Central Middle School. After the fire of 1916, they rebuilt the existing church there in 1917. In 1972, the new first United Methodist Church opened on North Territorial Road. This church has held several Christian denominations since then. The historic photograph was taken around 1915.

Cardinal Edward Mooney established St. John's Provincial Seminary in 1948, and it continued operations until 1988, when it closed. In 1996, the St. John's Center for Youth and Family opened. In 1998, work commenced on an $11 million redevelopment of the property into a comprehensive center for corporate and social conferences, Catholic weddings, and celebrations. October 2000 marked the grand opening of St. John's Golf and Conference Center, and the Inn at St. John's opened in 2006.

CHURCHES AND SCHOOLS

Ann Arbor Lutheran pastor Friedrich Schmid first began serving the Plymouth community in 1836. In 1855, the Plymouth congregation purchased the former Presbyterian and Baptist frame church house in Old Village and organized as St. Peter's Evangelical Lutheran Church in 1856. A larger church building was constructed at the end of Spring Street in Old Village in 1883. A two-room schoolhouse was built on Penniman Avenue in 1945. The present church building was built next door in 1955 (seen here).

St. John's Episcopal Church started with a group of six women in April 1898, as the Women's Guild of St. John's Mission. After disbanding in 1903, the commission was reorganized in 1912 with 12 members who met in the Universalist church at the corner of Dodge and Union Streets. The first permanent church was on Union Street. The church building later moved to the corner of Harvey and Maple Streets and finally to its present location on Sheldon Road in 1960 (seen here).

CHURCHES AND SCHOOLS

In 1970, ground-breaking ceremonies were held for the new First United Methodist Church, located on 15 acres on the south side of North Territorial Road. The new church was consecrated by the bishop on March 5, 1972 (seen here). In 1988, a $3.2 million expansion began with a new 600-seat sanctuary. It was completed in 1990. The former sanctuary is used for meeting rooms today.

Plymouth's first frame schoolhouse, called the seminary, was built here in 1840 and was donated to the village by prominent landowner and businessman Ebenezer Penniman. A brick schoolhouse replaced this building in 1884. That school and the Methodist church next door burnt down in 1916. Plymouth High School was rebuilt in 1917 on the same location (seen here in 1951). It was converted to Central Middle School in 1970 when the new Plymouth Salem High School opened in the township.

CHURCHES AND SCHOOLS

The park in front of Central Middle School was called Central Park in the early 1900s. The construction of the cobblestone wall surrounding the park in 1933 was part of Pres. Herbert Hoover's reconstruction finance program. In 2006, the Plymouth Community Veterans' Memorial Park opened here with all of Plymouth's war memorials. The majority of the construction funds for the park were raised through the 2004 sale of a veterans' house deeded by the Hough family to the veterans' foundation.

The Starkweather School was named after George Anson Starkweather, whose first occupation was a schoolteacher. The classic revival building was built in 1927 for $125,000 and served as a grade school from 1927 to 1977. Today it serves as an adult education center. The school was built in Old Village largely through the strong lobbying efforts of citizens in the area, who often felt slighted when it came to issues of municipal amenities.

CHURCHES AND SCHOOLS

TO MAKE A BUCK

This photograph of Charles Roe (left) and William Markham (right) was taken in the late 1920s at Markham's estate in Glendale, California. Roe and Markham are exemplary examples of Plymouth's entrepreneurial spirit. Roe was vice president and general manager for the Markham Air Rifle Company and has been credited by some for creating Markham's first wooden BB gun.

E. Gottlieb Bode built the Bode Hotel in 1868 on Main Street in anticipation of the coming railroads. The hotel later closed and was converted to a residence by George and Marguerite Hugar in 1927. It was also home to Nazarene Church in 1938. In 1959, Larry Gafka and Al Sequin established Bode's Corned Beef House here (seen in 1968). Current owners Pam and Richard Meachum have run the business since the 1960s.

In 1871, George Starkweather erected the building that contains today's Herman's Grille, one of the oldest standing commercial structures in Plymouth. At the time, Starkweather owned a general store on Main Street but thought it wise to move his business closer to the coming railroad depot on Oak Road (Starkweather Street). He built a new house across the street in 1875. The building shown here around 1880 contained, from left to right, John Meiler's drugs, Peter Gayde's grocery, and Starkweather's General Merchandise.

The Markham Air Rifle Company manufacturing plant, seen here around 1900, was added on to several times over the years. Only the far northern section remains today. William F. Markham is credited with creating the first successful BB gun. In 1886, he began manufacturing and selling a wooden, brass-barreled gun called the Challenger. Markham's success prompted the Plymouth Iron Windmill Company to become the Daisy Manufacturing Company in 1895 and begin competing head-to-head with Markham. Eventually Daisy bought out Markham in 1916.

In 1888, the Plymouth Iron Windmill Company began giving away an all-metal BB gun created by Clarence Hamilton. The popularity of the BB gun quickly overshadowed the windmills, and the company began solely selling BB guns in 1895, switching its name to Daisy Manufacturing Company (seen here around 1930). Daisy became the world leader in BB gun sales but left Plymouth in 1958 for Rogers, Arkansas, and a more modern factory. One lone wall on Union Street is all that remains today.

The E. L. Riggs General Store was established in 1894 in the newly rebuilt Phoenix Block on Main Street in front of Kellogg Park. It is seen here in 1900. Large advertisements appeared regularly in the *Plymouth Mail* newspaper for this general store in the early 1900s. This business block burned twice, in 1856 and 1893. This section of buildings is the oldest on Main Street, dating back to 1893 when they were reconstructed after the fire.

The Alter motorcar was designed by Clarence Alter of Manitowoc, Wisconsin. The car was made from component parts shipped to Plymouth by rail for assembly. Two models were produced, a five-passenger touring car and a roadster. Only one Alter is known to have survived, and it is on display at the Plymouth Historical Museum. Alter produced over 1,000 cars from 1914 to 1916 in this plant on Farmer Street (seen here around 1915) until closing its doors in January 1917.

The Schrader-Howell Funeral Home is Plymouth's second-oldest continuously operated business, established in 1904 by brothers Fred and Nelson Schrader (the oldest business, Heide's Flowers, was established in 1889). Their original business on Penniman Avenue moved to this former residence on Main Street in 1917. In 1991, third-generation family member Edwin (Win) Schrader merged the business with Patrick Lynch and Michael Howell of Lynch and Sons Funeral home to create Schrader-Howell Funeral Home. The Ellis Restaurant burned down in the 1970s (seen here in 1968).

The Plymouth Mail newspaper was founded in 1887 by J. H. Steers, and the original printing office was located on Sutton Street (Penniman Avenue) next to the Penniman-Allen Theater. Its new office opened on Main Street in 1924 (seen here). Under the Eaton family ownership from 1930 to 1952, the newspaper took on a greater social slant, publishing many notes and reports of the social activities of its citizens. It was purchased by Phillip Power in 1966 and absorbed into the Plymouth Observer newspapers.

This former Ford village factory was built in 1923 on the site of the former Wilcox Mill (Wilcox Road and Hines Drive) and maintained operations through 1948 when it was sold to the Wayne County Road Commission. Henry Ford built over 30 village industries plants in an experiment of decentralized rural plants, making parts and other components for Ford vehicles—all located on the banks of rivers to take advantage of hydroelectric power. The Plymouth Ford plant made taps for Ford's big Rouge plant.

The former Independent Telephone Company/Michigan Bell building was constructed in 1926. The first telephone toll station in Plymouth was at John Gale's drugstore at the corner of Main Street and Penniman Avenue in 1886. In the early days, several competing small telephone companies emerged in Plymouth. Edward Hough of Daisy acclaim, Charles Fisher, Dr. Taft, and Chauncey Rauch created the Plymouth Telephone Company in 1891, and Hough held telephone number one for 65 years before the extension format was changed.

Hotel Mayflower, Plymouth, Mich.

The southwest corner of Main Street and Ann Arbor Trail was the location of Plymouth's first home. The city's first settlers, William and Kezia Starkweather, built a shack of saplings and bark here on March 11, 1825. This same corner also was the location of the stately brick home of Mr. and Mrs. John Fuller (she was daughter of Plymouth pioneer John Kellogg.) The Mayflower Hotel operated here from 1927 through 1999 (seen here about 1930), and the Mayflower Centre was built in 2000.

Herman Bakhaus opened a dairy bottling plant in Plymouth in 1933 and in 1948 opened a retail store and bottling plant on the site of today's 1999 Tavern on Forest Avenue. Cloverdale's quickly became a favorite hangout for teens and the cruising crowds of the 1950s (seen here about 1953) as well as a place for family gatherings up until its closing. Bakhaus sold the business in 1974 to the Tomlinson family, and the business closed its doors for good in 1992.

In 1947, Margaret Dunning purchased Goldstein's Apparel on Main Street in Plymouth and renamed the store Dunning's. In 1950, she moved Dunning's department store to Forest Avenue where E. G. Nick's restaurant stands today. She sold the store in 1968 to Minerva Chaiken, and it became known as Minerva's–Dunning's (seen here). Chaiken previously owned Minerva's dress shop on Penniman Avenue next to the Penniman-Allen Theater, which burned down in 1968. Minerva's–Dunning's closed in 1997 when Chaiken retired.

This popular Plymouth ice-cream parlor first opened as a Dairy Queen in 1950 and switched names to Dairy King in 1973 (seen here). The Lang family purchased the business in 1976 and constructed the current building. In 1999, Michael and Mary Hurley of Plymouth purchased the business and have continued the tradition as Plymouth's affordable treat and family gathering spot. Many Plymouth teenagers can claim Dairy King as their first job.

The location of today's Plymouth Independence Village retirement community (opened in 1998) was once home to the Calvacade Inn, Thunderbird Inn, Thunderbird Hilton Inn, and Plymouth Raddison Hotel. The Calvacade Inn burned down in 1957 and was replaced by the Thunderbird Inn. In 1976, a five-story 195-room Hilton addition was built in anticipation of a new interstate exit at Northville Road, which never materialized. The hotel later rebranded as the Plymouth Raddison Hotel for a short while before closing altogether.

4

STREETS, ROADS, AND TRAILS

This is Main Street looking north across from Central Middle School around 1950. Main Street was first paved with bricks in 1908. Until then, it was often criticized due to the mud and ruts that came about as a result of heavy horse-and-buggy traffic and the ravages of changing seasons.

This is a view of Main Street from the 1940s looking north at Ann Arbor Trail. The Mayflower Coffee House inside the hotel, south of here and out of view, is where many of the city's power brokers and common citizens met. On the opposite corner sat the D and C five-and-dime store, which opened in the 1940s and closed in the 1960s. Parkside Gallery occupies that same corner building today.

This view of a Fourth of July parade was taken from the top of the Mayflower Hotel in the 1950s. The parade used to proceed on a northerly route. Today it takes a southerly route and starts at 7:00 a.m.—the earliest in the state. The angled parking in front of Kellogg Park, the S. S. Kresge store, and the large building on the right at the corner of Main Street and Penniman Avenue are all vestiges of Plymouth's past.

This is a closer view of the S. S. Kresge department store building in the 1950s, soon after the former structures dating from 1893 were razed (see page 68). Sebastian Spering Kresge (1867–1966) founded the S. S. Kresge Company (later Kmart) in 1899, now part of the Sears Holdings Corporation. This store was later closed in the 1960s when the new Kmart was built on Ann Arbor Road. The popular Little Professor bookstore preceded today's Fiamma Grill in this location.

This view is from the early 1900s on Main Street looking north from Church Street. The large house on the right is still standing today but is hidden inside the commercial building located at 127 South Main Street. Built about 1870, the house was once owned by Fred Schrader, founder of Schrader's Funeral Home, and then his son Edwin until 1959. After that, it became home to the Cadillac Drapery store. A new brick storefront was added in the late 1960s.

It is hard to believe that these two photographs are of the same location. Most of Main Street contained beautiful, large houses except for the commercial section in front of Kellogg Park. The high banks were created in 1908 when Main Street was leveled and paved with brick, over the protests of many homeowners here. Commercial development and road widening over the years has removed the extreme grade change shown in the early photograph from about 1910.

This spot once marked the divide between Plymouth's developed and rural existence. Much of this land was once owned by the Shattuck family. At the top of the hill on the south side of Plymouth Road sat the Streng family farmhouse (built 1908), which was later converted to the Hillside Inn (today's Ernesto's Italian Garden) by Jacob and Margaret (Streng) Stremich in 1934. The name changed to Ernesto's in the late 1980s. The historic photograph was taken around 1920.

This tree lined, two-lane road is not one of Plymouth's residential streets but is Main Street looking south at today's Central Middle School around 1930. The curb recess on the immediate right was a drop-off/pick-up location for students. The road changed dramatically when the city widened North Main Street in 1956 and South Main Street 1958, due to increased traffic and congestion. The loss of many large trees and the "small-town Main Street" feel angered many Plymouth citizens.

STREETS, ROADS, AND TRAILS

This view from around 1900 of Main Street shows hitching posts in front of Kellogg Park and the 1893 Coleman building on the immediate right, which preceded the bank seen today. The bandstand in Kellogg Park was removed in the early 1920s. Wooden sidewalks made their appearance in Plymouth in 1872 and concrete ones in 1891. Main Street was not paved with brick, however, until 1908. The interurban train track can be seen turning left onto Sutton Street (Penniman Avenue).

This view of the southern section of the Kellogg Park business block (built in 1893) dates from around 1950, before it was torn down to make way for the S. S. Kresge store in 1951. A Kroger grocery store occupied the redbrick building to the right of the parked trailer in the 1930s and 1940s. Wiltse's Pharmacy (established by Pat Wiltse in 1936) is visible on the immediate right in the historic photograph.

This view of West Ann Arbor Trail looking toward town west of Evergreen is from the 1930s. On the right is the stately brick house of Edward Hough (built 1918). Hough was the son of Daisy Manufacturing Company founder, Lewis Cass Hough, and was Daisy's longtime vice president and treasurer before serving as its president from 1956 until his death in 1959. He was responsible for developing the Hough Park subdivision in 1926 on his family's property and woods.

This view of West Ann Arbor Trail looking toward Harvey Street is from the 1950s. Ann Arbor Trail was called Ann Arbor Street until 1934. This road was initially a Native American trail that ran along the Rouge River. In 1826, Bethuel Farrand gathered the help of area men and cleared this wagon road from Ann Arbor through Plymouth and into Detroit in 60 days.

The historic photograph shows the interurban streetcar tracks being laid in 1898 on Ann Arbor Trail near the east–west railroad tracks. The interurban ran from 1898 to 1924, and passengers could travel around the greater-Detroit area through a series of multiowned lines and depots. This track ran from Northville down Northville Road onto Mill Street where it turned south onto Main Street toward downtown, headed east down Penniman Avenue in front of Kellogg Park, and then onto Ann Arbor Trail heading east toward Wayne.

A Kroger grocery store once occupied the building that houses Blue Moon Music and Heidi's Old Village Flowers today. Heidi's is the oldest business in Plymouth, established by Carl Heidi in 1899 as Heidi's Greenhouse, originally located at the southeast corner of Liberty and Mill Streets. Heidi sold the business in 1939, and the greenhouse side of the enterprise was eliminated in 1974. The owners and location of the business has changed several times, but the name has remained constant. The historic photograph was taken around 1920.

The St. Michael's Melkite Catholic Church is located on the west side of North Mill Street, south of Liberty Street. Built in 1856 and later remodeled, this is the oldest church still standing in Plymouth. It was originally the First Baptist Church (seen here about 1905) until 1968 when the congregation moved to its new church on North Territorial Road. The house in front of the church was built about 1900 and is used for commercial purposes today.

Peter Gayde, an emigrant from Wuerttemberg, Germany, started his cooper business in Plymouth in 1854 in the south wing of his home. In 1871, Gayde established a store, called Peter Gayde's Grocery and Provision, with two of his sons in the Starkweather building on Liberty Street (far building). In 1895, Gayde's third son, William, opened his own butcher shop just a few doors down from the Gayde Brothers Grocery Store (seen here), which operated until 1946.

STREETS, ROADS, AND TRAILS

This view of Penniman Avenue, looking east toward Main Street from Harvey Street, shows how Sutton Street (Penniman Avenue) was once lined with beautiful houses. The first two houses in the historic photograph from about 1900 are still standing today; the second house on the left is the Coffee Bean. The third house on the left burned down in 1996 and is now the empty lot next to the Coffee Bean. Sutton Street was renamed Penniman Avenue in 1918.

The buildings in the 1950s photograph containing D. Galin and Sons Appliances, the Penniman-Allen Theater, Minerva's dress shop, and Sandy's Drugs burned down in 1968—only the three window, two-story building in the foreground survived (today's Haven home décor store). The buildings were replaced by condominiums and retail shops in 2005. The Penniman-Allen Theater was built in 1918 by Kate (Penniman) Allen, daughter of Plymouth pioneer Ebenezer Penniman. She was a successful businesswoman and is responsible for developing the commercial section of Penniman Avenue.

A large building (seen here around 1950) occupied the northeast corner of Penniman Avenue and Main Street from the late 1800s through 1962, when it was demolished along with the three other buildings to make way for the new First Federal Bank (today's Charter One Bank). There were some residences on this section of Penniman Avenue in the early years, but it has primarily contained commercial enterprises. The Gathering covered parking, east of the Penn Theater, was built in 1984.

Sutton Street (Penniman Avenue) had two-way traffic most of its existence. The historic photograph dates from the early 1920s, soon after the Plymouth United Savings Bank was built in 1920. An Edison electric light pole stands in the middle of the photograph. The Conner building on the right (built 1898) takes it namesake from Michael Conner, whose hardware store was at this corner from 1857 to 1961.

STREETS, ROADS, AND TRAILS

The 1930s view of commercial buildings on Penniman Avenue shows some familiar names from Plymouth's past, including Davis and Lent's Men's Wear (which moved to Main Street in the 1960s), Huston and Company Hardware (existing from the late 1800s to 1961), and Blunk's Furniture (existing from 1913 to 1961). Blunk's became Schrader's Furniture, and the Blunks then opened an electronics store on Starkweather Street. The First National Bank was established in 1924 and operated until 1952. The Penniman-Allen Theater, built by Kate (Penniman) Allen operated from 1918 to 1968.

Jack Holloway stands with his horse in front of Park Livery around 1876. The last two houses on the right with the towers still stand today with the first one being the Coffee Bean. Harry Robinson, who owned the house at 865 Sutton Street, purchased the livery and also started a horse-and-carriage bus service. Livery stables boarded horses for a fee and were a staple in every town before the advent of the automobile.

STREETS, ROADS, AND TRAILS

Sheldon Road (seen here about 1955) was originally named Moreland Avenue after the Moreland family, who owned property nearby. Moreland Avenue originally commenced at Ann Arbor Trail and ran north. Sheldon Road commenced at Ann Arbor Road and ran south. The two roads were connected in the late 1930s, and the Moreland portion was renamed Sheldon Road in 1956. Sheldon Road derives its name from Timothy and Rachael Sheldon, who established the Sheldon Inn in Canton in the 1820s.

The intersection of Church Street and Harvey Street has been home to residences since the dawn of the 20th century, as can be seen from this early-1900s photograph. The Penniman family owned most of the land in this area, and Will and Kate (Penniman) Allen are responsible for the majority of its residential development between 1900 and 1920. All of these houses are still standing today, with the closest one on the right no longer having the wrap-around porch.

STREETS, ROADS, AND TRAILS

The early photograph of Blunk Street looking north from Church Street was taken around 1925. The small trees along the boulevard have grown to become the tree-canopied street seen today. William Blunk (1860–1938) was born in Temple, Germany, and came to America in 1886. In 1913, Blunk purchased 40 acres of land in Plymouth, which he developed as the Blunk subdivision (bounded by Sheldon Road and Junction, and Harvey and Church/William Streets). Blunk's first home here was built in 1907 at 1012 William Street.

This late-1930s photograph of William Street looking north shows a very developed Ann Street. All of the houses except for three between William and Blanch Streets were built between 1915 and 1927. Several streets in this area are named after the Blunk family, including William and Blunk, named for William Blunk; Arthur and Irvin (Irving), named after two of William's sons; and Ann, relation unknown. Blunks's sons owned Blunk's Furniture on Penniman Avenue and Blunk's Electronics on Starkweather Street.

In 1964, the old city hall (white building, built in 1880) was razed, and Church Street was cut through to Union Street. The new city hall was built at the new intersection of Main and Church Streets. The building to the right of the old city hall is the Christian Scientist Church (built in 1903), which was sold to the city and razed for this project. The congregation then relocated to its new church building on Ann Arbor Trail (for sale in 2009).

The early Charles Draper photograph from about 1900, taken close to his house on Church Street, shows Penniman-Allen Park located at the point where the west end of Church Street connects into Penniman Avenue. Plymouth Historical Society president emeritus Sanford Burr recalls as a child watching the band play inside the bandstand here, as Kate (Penniman) Allen's guests arrived for one of her many social affairs at the Penniman-Allen house. The house that occupies the point today was built in 1989.

CHAPTER 5

THIS, THAT, AND WHATNOT

The Plymouth Fair Association was organized in 1886, and the first fair was held that same year. The fairgrounds stood on 22 acres south of Ann Arbor Trail near its intersection with Fairground Street and were surrounded by a high-board fence. The fair was closed in 1903, and houses started appearing just before 1920. A family admission ticket cost $1.

This is a view of Kellogg Park from about 1905 from East Ann Arbor Trail looking toward Main Street. In 1972, Union Street was cut through the apex of the park to connect to Ann Arbor Trail. Penniman Avenue, which used to run in front of the Markham-Wilcox house to Ann Arbor Trail, was terminated at Union Street. The land in front of the Markham-Wilcox house was filled in and landscaped. A new fountain and brick walkways were also added to the park.

Kellogg Park has been home to fairs and festivals since its inception. This view from the early 1900s, when contrasted with the present view from the 2009 Green Street Fair, shows the evolution of "casual attire" over a century. Except for Main Street, and portions of Sutton (Penniman Avenue), Kellogg Park was primarily surrounded by residences in the early years.

Plymouth, Mich.

The original parcel of land containing today's Penn Theater was purchased by the Woodward Theatre Company from George Wilcox in 1926. Harry Lush, employed by the Penniman and Allen Theater, bought the still-vacant land in 1939 to build his own theater. It opened in 1941 and was named in honor of his recently deceased friend and former employer, Kate (Penniman) Allen. After closing in 2003, a small group of local philanthropists bought the Penn Theater in 2005, saving it from demolition.

The early photograph shows the Ann Arbor Trail/Main Street intersection and the Mayflower Hotel in the 1940s. The monument shown here honored those Plymouth men who fought in World War II. The monument was temporary and was later removed with the names of those men now appearing on one of the monuments at the Plymouth Community Veterans' Memorial Park in front of Central Middle School. The Mayflower Hotel was razed in 2000 to make way for the new Mayflower Centre.

The soldiers' monument honoring those men who fought in the "war between the states, 1861 to 1865," was given to the city by Harry Bradner in 1917 and was originally located in Kellogg Park. In 1968, attorney Perry Richwine donated money to move the monument to Riverside Cemetery as part of a Kellogg Park beautification project. The monument was moved to its current location in 2006 as part of the Plymouth Community Veterans' Memorial Park project in front of Central Middle School.

Riverside Cemetery, Plymouth, Mich.

Riverside Cemetery was established in 1880 on property purchased by the Village of Plymouth from Franklin and Ellen Shattuck in 1877 (seen here about 1915). Plymouth's first cemetery, established in 1835, stood beneath today's Presbyterian church parking lot. The bodies were later moved to Riverside Cemetery in 1915 and 1916. The city's oldest-standing cemetery is the Old Baptist Cemetery, established 1845 at York and Pearl Streets. Shearer Cemetery on North Territorial Road in the township, was established in 1826.

Plymouth's first train depot was built in 1871 when the railroads came to town (seen here in 1910). Pere Marquette owned both of the tracks that crossed Plymouth from about 1900 through the 1920s. The Chesapeake and Ohio Railway gained ownership in 1947, and it merged with the Chessie System in 1972, which became part of CSX in 1980. The railroads aided the early Plymouth economy by providing a convenient distribution network for local farmers and a growing manufacturing base.

THIS, THAT, AND WHATNOT